Your Success As A CIO Depends On How Well You Communicate

Tips And Techniques For CIOs To Use In Order To Become Better Communicators

"Practical, proven techniques that will help you to make your CIO career long and successful"

Dr. Jim Anderson

Published by:
Blue Elephant Consulting
Tampa, Florida

Copyright © 2016 by Dr. Jim Anderson

All rights reserved. No part of this book may be reproduced of transmitted in any form or by any means, electronic or mechanical, including photocopying, recording or by any information storage and retrieval system without written permission of the publisher, except for inclusion of brief quotations in a review.

Printed in the United States of America

Library of Congress Control Number: 2016913064

ISBN-13: 978-1536987218

ISBN-10: 1536987212

Warning – Disclaimer

The purpose of this book is to educate and entertain. This book does not promise or guarantee that anyone following the ideas, tips, suggestions, techniques or strategies will be successful. The author, publisher and distributor(s) shall have neither liability nor responsibility to anyone with respect to any loss or damage caused, or alleged to be caused, directly or indirectly by the information contained in this book.

Other Books By The Author

Product Management

- How To Have A Successful Product Manager Career: The Things That You Need To Be Doing TODAY In Order To Have A Successful Product Manager Career

- Product Manager Product Success: How to keep your product on track and make it become a success

Public Speaking

- How To Create A Speech That Will Be Remembered

- Secrets To Planning The Perfect Speech

CIO Skills

- CIO Business Skills: How CIOs can work effectively with the rest of the company!

- Managing Your CIO Career: Steps That CIOs Have To Take In Order To Have A Long And Successful Career

IT Manager Skills

- IT Manager Budgeting Skills

- IT Manager Career Secrets: Tips And Techniques That IT Managers Can Use In Order To Have A Successful Career

Negotiating

- Preparing For Your Next Negotiation: What You Need To Do BEFORE A Negotiation Starts In Order To Get The Best Possible Deal

- How To Open Your Next Negotiation: How To Start A Negotiation In Order To Get The Best Possible Outcome

Miscellaneous

- Power Distribution Unit (PDU) Secrets: What Everyone Who Works In A Data Center Needs To Know!

- Making The Jump: How To Land Your Dream Job When You Get Out Of College!

Acknowledgements

Any book like this one is the result of years of real-world work experience. In my over 25 years of working for 7 different firms, I have met countless fantastic people and I've been mentored by some truly exceptional ones. Although I've probably forgotten some of the people who made me the person that I am today, here is my attempt to finally give them the recognition that they so truly deserve:

- Thomas P. Anderson
- Art Puett
- Bobbi Marshall
- Bob Boggs

Dr. Jim Anderson

This book is dedicated to my wife Lori. None of this would have been possible without her love and support.

Thanks for the best 21 years of my life (so far)...!

Table Of Contents

CIOS WHO COMMUNICATE THE BEST ARE THE MOST SUCCESSFUL ...8

ABOUT THE AUTHOR 10

CHAPTER 1: CIOS SHOULD STOP SENDING EMAILS – NOW! 15

CHAPTER 2: CIO LESSONS FROM ZYNGA: DON'T MANAGE LIKE THEY DO! 19

CHAPTER 3: WHAT A CIO NEEDS TO KNOW ABOUT CREATING A TWITTER STRATEGY 24

CHAPTER 4: WHY CIOS NEED TO DISCOVER IT PARADISE BY THE DASHBOARD LIGHTS 28

CHAPTER 5: HOW CIOS CAN MAKE SOCIAL MEDIA WORK FOR THEM, NOT AGAINST THEM 32

CHAPTER 6: CIOS NEED TO HELP WORKERS TO "LIKE" THEIR JOBS MORE 36

CHAPTER 7: 5 SECRETS A CIO NEEDS TO KNOW IN ORDER TO CREATE A SOCIAL MEDIA PLAN 41

CHAPTER 8: 5 WAYS THAT CIOS CAN DO A BETTER JOB OF COMMUNICATING IN THE OFFICE 45

CHAPTER 9: 3 TIPS FOR CIOS TO BECOME BETTER NEGOTIATORS 49

CHAPTER 10: HOW CAN CIOS COMMAND THE ROOM DURING A SPEECH? 52

CHAPTER 11: HOW THE ORANGE COUNTY CTO SOLVED HIS IT PROBLEM 56

CHAPTER 12: HOW CIOS CAN USE WORDS TO BOOST THEIR POWER AND CREDIBILITY 60

CIOs Who Communicate The Best Are The Most Successful

When we think about what it takes to be a successful CIO, there are a lot of things that probably come to mind. Staying on top of changing technology, anticipating security issues, and preparing the IT department for the company's growth. However, it turns out that there is something that is far more important than any of these things to a CIO's success: the ability to clearly communicate.

One of the first things that any CIO needs to understand is that email is not their friend. It is a powerful tool, but it can be overused. We need to look at different companies and see what they are doing correctly – and wrong. We are living in the age of social media and as the company's CIO you are going to have to find ways to make these tools work for you, not against you.

When it comes to social media, because there are now so many different tools, a CIO is going to have to take the time to create a plan for how to maximize the value of each tool. At the same time it is going to be the CIOs responsibility to make sure that each of the members of the IT department feel satisfied in their job. To make this happen, the CIO is going to have to become a good communicator in the office.

Communication can take on many different forms for a CIO. One of the more common forms is that of negotiation. No matter if it is with workers, other departments, or vendors this is a skill that every CIO needs to have. Another communication skill that a CIO has to have is the ability to give a speech to a room full of people. This can be tricky to do well, but as with all such things, it is something that can be learned with practice.

The job of CIO is something that is being done every day at just about every company. As CIO we need to understand that we can learn from the experiences that our peers have had and we can adopt some of their strategies inside of our companies. When we go to communicate with our teams and peers we'll have to keep in mind that the words that we choose to use will determine how much power and credibility we will be given.

The good news about communication for CIOs is that this is a skill that can be learned. If we're willing to take the time and commit ourselves to becoming better communicators, then we can become more successful CIOs.

For more information on what it takes to be a great CIO, check out my blog, The Accidental Successful CIO, at:

www.TheAccidentalSuccessfulCIO.com

Good luck!

- Dr. Jim Anderson

About The Author

I must confess that I never set out to be a CIO. When I went to school, I studied Computer Science and thought that I'd get a nice job programming and that would be that. Well, at least part of that plan worked out!

My first job was working for Boeing on their F/A-18 fighter jet program. I spent my days programming fighter jet software in assembly language and I loved it. The U.S. government decided to save some money and went looking for other countries to sell this plane to. This put me into an unfamiliar role: I started to meet with foreign military officials and I ended up having to manage groups of engineers who were working on international projects.

Time moved on and so did I. I found myself working for Siemens, the big German telecommunications company. They were making phone switches and selling them to the seven U.S. phone companies. The problem was that the switches were too complicated. Customers couldn't tell the difference between one complicated phone switch from another complicated phone switch. Once again I found myself working with the sales and marketing teams to find ways to make the great technology that the engineers had developed understandable to both internal and external customers.

I've spent over 25 years working as an senior IT professional for both big companies and startups. This has given me an opportunity to learn what it takes to manage and IT department in ways that allow it to maximize its output while becoming a valuable part of the overall company.

I now live in Tampa Florida where I spend my time managing my consulting business, Blue Elephant Consulting, teaching college courses at the University of South Florida, and traveling to work with companies like yours to share the knowledge that I have about how to create and manage successful IT departments.

I'm always available to answer questions and I can be reached at:

Dr. Jim Anderson
Blue Elephant Consulting
Email: jim@BlueElephantConsulting.com
Facebook: http://goo.gl/1TVoK
Web: http://www.BlueElephantConsulting.com/

"Unforgettable communication skills that will set your ideas free..."

Create IT Departments That Are Productive And A Valuable Asset To The Rest Of The Company !

Dr. Jim Anderson is available to provide training and coaching on the topics that are the most important to people who have to manage IT departments: how can I build a productive IT department (and keep it together) while at the same time providing the rest of the company with the IT services that they need?

Dr. Anderson believes that in order to both learn and remember what he says, speakers need to laugh. Each one of his speeches is full of fun and humor so that what he says "sticks" with everyone.

Dr. Anderson's CIO SkillsTraining Includes:

1. How to identify and attract the right type of IT workers to your IT department.
2. How to build relationships with the company's senior management in order to get the support that you need?
3. How to stay on top of changing technology and security issues so that you never get surprised?

Dr. Jim Anderson works with over 100 customers per year. To invite Dr. Anderson to work with you, contact him at:

Phone: 813-418-6970 or
Email: jim@BlueElephantConsulting.com

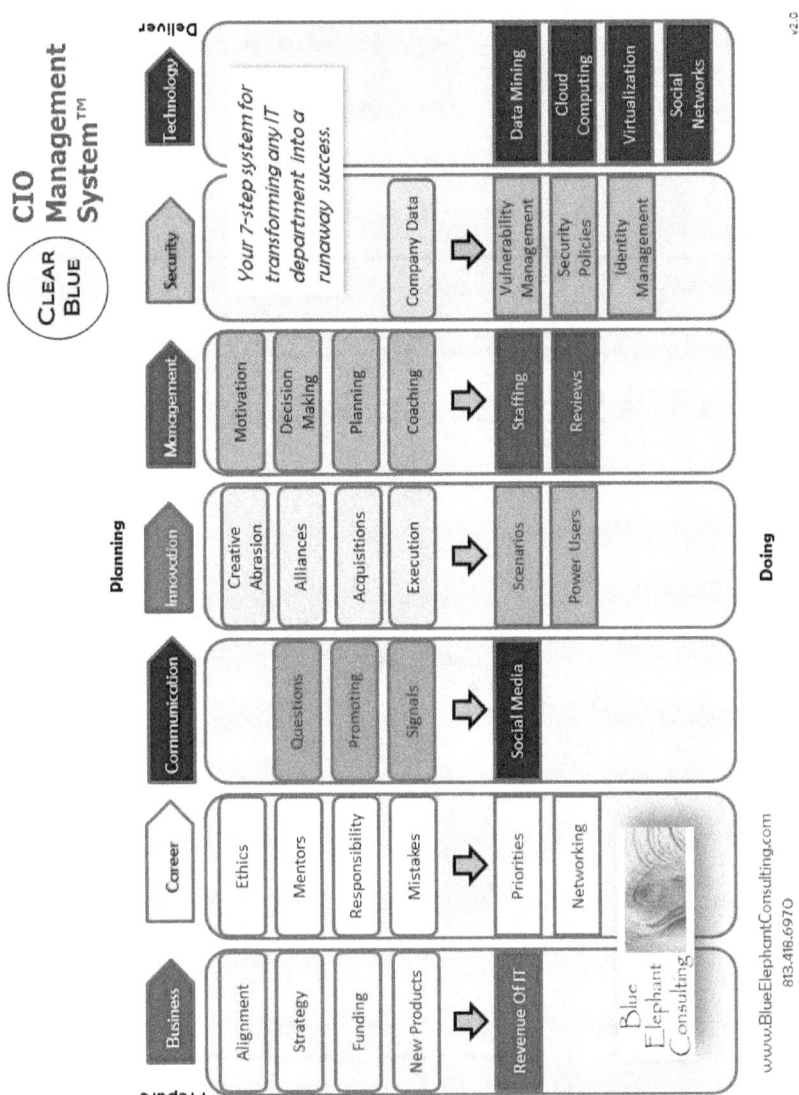

The Clear Blue CIO Management System™ has been created to provide CIOs and senior IT managers with a clear roadmap for how to manage an IT department. This system shows CIOs what needs to be done and in what order to do it.

Chapter 1

CIOs Should Stop Sending Emails – Now!

Chapter 1: CIOs Should Stop Sending Emails – Now!

Those cloning experiments sure seem to have only been able to create more sheep so far – and that's not going to help overworked CIOs! It seems as though we have **more things to do and less time than ever to get them done**. Arguably the most important part of any CIOs job is to communicate with your staff. How you go about doing that can be critical to both your overall success and the success of your IT department. I've got news for you: if you're using email to do this, then you're doing it wrong.

Email Has No Feeling

I don't care how much of a cold and impersonal CIO you are. Every time that you talk with someone, **you include some level of emotions in what you are saying**. You may be angry, you may be happy, no matter what – you are something.

The problem with email is that it's nothing. Your emails are never happy, sad, or mad. The person that you've sent your email to **can't tell what you were feeling** when you wrote your email.

What this means is that **the possibility of a miscommunication** skyrockets when we use email. Since we can't properly let the reader of our email know how we were feeling when we wrote the email, the possibility of getting signals mixed up is very probable.

Email Creates Negative Responses

What do you do when you read an email that has been sent to you? I'm willing to bet that more often than not, **you jot off a**

quick reply to the sender right then and there. Without giving it a lot of thought.

Things get even more tricky when we get negative emails – someone yelling at us or complaining about something. What happens is that we get bent out of shape and our anger wells up inside of us and then comes rushing out through our fingertips as we type out **that heated email** that we're going to send back.

We all know what the right thing to do here is (even if we don't always do it). When we get an email that makes us mad, we really need to **stand up and walk away**. Don't reply to that email right off the bat. In fact, if at all possible, don't reply to it today – wait a day. That will allow everything to cool down and you'll be able to craft a reply that you won't regret later on.

Email Creates Debates That Are Not Needed

Because of the anonymous nature of email and because we really can't figure out what the other people are thinking, **debates can go on and on**. It's very hard to stop a debate once it's stated via email.

Miscommunication and the simple fact that it's so easy to just flip another email back to the sender **contribute to this problem**. Even after the primary issue has been resolved, the discussion can go on and on as both parties continue to explore.

Debates are one of the key communication areas that are **not well served by email**. The back-and-forth nature of this type of communication along with the need to "see" what the other side really means results in the need for face-to-face contact.

What All Of This Means For You

Look, email is a great tool. I use it, you use it, everybody in the IT sector uses it. The use of email is probably included in definition of information technology. The key is to not **over use it** or use it in the wrong situations. CIOs need to be able to identify when and where the correct times to use emails are.

Email has **three distinct problems** associated with it. First, it does a lousy job of communicating emotion and this can lead to confusion on the part of the receiver of your email. Next it can cause people to become instantly angry – they don't take the time to think about what they've read before they fire off a response. Finally, email makes it too easy to keep talking about an issue long after it should have been put to bed.

I'm not suggesting that CIOs stop using email. Far from it. Rather, I'd actually like to see CIOs use email as **their communication technique of last resort**. The importance of information technology is so great that you need to pick up the phone or walk over to someone's office instead of firing off that next email. You just might end up being glad that you did!

Chapter 2

CIO Lessons From Zynga: Don't Manage Like They Do!

Chapter 2: CIO Lessons From Zynga: Don't Manage Like They Do!

Just in case you've been living under a rock for the past year and don't know who Zynga is, they're **the online game company** that has ridden Facebook's coattails to success. They've created very, very popular games such as Farmville and Cityville and generated a great deal of money. However, it's starting to become clear that Zynga is not very well run internally and this holds many lessons for CIOs...

What's Wrong With Zynga

How would you like your staff to be **describing your IT department** in the following ways:

- "Poor leadership and communication. Awful work-life balance."

- "Being told by my manager that if i am not at home sleeping, then i am here working. That is how i was welcomed to the team."

- "Long hours even when there is no real deadline. Insane micromanagement all the way from CEO down"

These are **actual quotes** from (supposedly) Zynga employees that have been posted at the workplace rating site glassdoor.com. Ouch! What's wrong with Zynga?

It's pretty clear that Zynga is experiencing a massive surge of growth and they're not exactly sure how deal with it. As the company grows and grows, the folks who are running the show are desperately trying deal with all of the business issues and appear to be forgetting what makes a company succeed over the long haul: **its people**.

We've all see this happen in many IT departments. When the department was small, there were a few people working in it who **developed a close working relationship**. Everything could be handled by someone in the department and there was an understanding that everyone would do whatever it took in order to get things done.

Where things **start to go off the track** is when the department grows. It doesn't matter if the growth is organic (the business grows so the IT department grows) or through acquisitions. When the rules and understanding that were in place for that small group of people is extended to cover a larger group, **this starts to cause problems**.

It's pretty clear that the folks running Zynga's IT shop haven't taken the time to craft **a new set of policies** that meet the needs of their growing team. This could quickly come back and bite them in the future.

How A Good CIO Could Fix What's Wrong At Zynga

It's easy to throw rocks at any organization and especially easy when it's growing as fast as Zynga is. Instead of doing that, how about if we step back for a moment and see if we can come up with a way that Zynga **could fix the mess that they've made**.

The first step would be to notify the staff that **you've made a mistake**. Letting everyone know that you've heard how unhappy they are and that you admit that you've screwed up is a huge thing to admit. By making this simple but hard to do gesture all of a sudden you'll have everyone's attention – normally nobody ever admits that they are wrong!

Next you've got to lay out some very clear goals for the Zynga teams to focus on. **What's most important?** Right now it's pretty clear that nobody quite knows. Is it being profitable? Is it having the most creative games? Is it reliability in the face of unheard of usage? There's no wrong answer here, you just need to pick one.

Finally, you've got to work with the front line managers and come up with **a standard set of rules** for how the IT workers are going to be evaluated. What's really important? Is it the quality of the products that folks are producing? Is it time spent in the office? Is it the quantity of the products that are being produced?

So much of Zynga's problems seem to stem from **poor communications** from the top on down. This probably wasn't necessary when the team was smaller. However, now that they've grown both how and what they communicate and good communication has become critically important.

What All Of This Means For You

What does this mess at Zynga mean for you? Although you probably don't currently work at Zynga, **you can learn from what's going on there**.

It's pretty clear that the Zynga IT workers are experiencing some serious **growing pains**. The reasons for these pains are well understood: the use of outdated processes coupled with poor internal communication has resulted in the situation that Zynga now finds itself in.

Just realizing that there is a problem is not enough. Instead, you need to understand **how a situation like this could be fixed**. Taking three steps that included apologizing, creating goals, and setting performance measurements would move the organization in the right direction.

With a little luck the Zynga CIO will get the message. Hopefully, they'll be able to make the changes that the company needs **before it's "game over"** for Zynga.

Chapter 3

What A CIO Needs To Know About Creating A Twitter Strategy

Chapter 3: What A CIO Needs To Know About Creating A Twitter Strategy

Is Twitter for real? I mean, is this going to be another one of those social media things that springs up, is hot-hot-hot for a bit, and then fades away and is forgotten? I don't have a crystal ball and so I can't tell you if Twitter has any staying power, but as a company's CIO in addition to running the IT department you are going to have to help **come up with the company's Twitter strategy**...

The Danger That Lurks In Tweets

So what's the big deal? Sure, sure we've all heard about Twitter, but isn't it just another one of **those social media tools** that is always lurking in the background in the IT sector but which really doesn't mean very much? You don't have to worry about this because it's not a part of the definition of information technology, right? Actually, you'd be wrong there.

It turns out that Twitter has exploded on the social media scene. Lots and lots of folks use Twitter to communicate – **27 million at last count**. What this means is that if your company starts to use Twitter as a way to connect with its customers, things can get out of hand very quickly.

Examples of cases where a company's "tweets" (postings using Twitter) **have gone wrong** are starting to multiply. Kenneth Cole Productions got into trouble when they tweeted that Egyptian protesters were taking to the streets because the company's new collection was available online. Chrysler Group ended up firing the agency that had been handling their Twitter account after someone made a disparaging post about how people in Detroit drive. The list goes on, but you get the point.

How Other Companies Have Handled This Issue

Realizing that this new Twitter tool **is a double-edged blade** is an important first step for CIOs. What you need to do next is to come up with a way for the company to effectively use it while at the same time making sure that the company does not shoot itself in its foot.

The first thing that a CIO can do is to work with the rest of the company to **determine just exactly who has access to the company's Twitter account**. For firms of any substantial size, this job could easily be bigger than just one person can handle. However, you want to keep the number relatively small (say no more than 10) so that you can have some control over what gets tweeted.

The next thing that you're going to have to work out is **just exactly how the company is going to want to use its Twitter account**. Are you going to be responding to customer complaints? If so, then you'll probably want to make contact with the complainer and take the discussion off of Twitter quickly.

No matter exactly how you choose to set up the company's Twitter team, **training is going to be important**. Because Twitter is one of those tools that crosses the boundary from our private lives into our work lives now, it's important that workers be trained – something that Best Buy does for all of their tweeting employees. Things that they might say or do on their private Twitter accounts might not be appropriate to say on the company's account. Yes, you want the company's tweets to be edgy and smart, but perhaps not THAT edgy...

What All Of This Means For You

When a CIO starts to deal with the question of how the company should handle its Twitter activities, **he or she is on a slippery slope**. Yes, Twitter is a fantastic way for the company to deepen its relationship with its customers; however, it can get out of hand quickly.

The CIO needs to help the company understand what issues it is going to have to deal with. The first is to determine **how many people should have access to the account**. The next is to determine just exactly what types of information the company should send out via Twitter.

There is always the possibility that Twitter might just be another flash-in-the-pan social media fad. However, right now it's looking that it might be **in for the long haul** and may end up contributing to the importance of information technology. CIOs need to step up and show some IT leadership by helping the company to establish a set of rules around how they want to use this powerful communication tool. Get it right, and your tweets will work for you, not against you...

Chapter 4

Why CIOs Need To Discover IT Paradise By The Dashboard Lights

Chapter 4: Why CIOs Need To Discover IT Paradise By The Dashboard Lights

Every once in a while a new idea comes along that is actually a pretty good idea. The **tsunami of data** that every company is currently trying to deal with has resulted in CFOs coming to the IT department and asking for help. Since in many cases the CIO works for the CFO, you had better be able to solve this data overload problem and do it quick!

What Do Dashboards Do For A Company?

So why all the excitement over dashboards in the IT sector? The driver behind the current wave of interest in data dashboards is pretty simple – everyone is overwhelmed by the information that is crossing their desk and they are desperately looking for ways to understand what it all means. Since data is at the heart of the definition of information technology, this sure looks like a job for the IT department to solve. Senior executives in your company are looking to a formal, integrated dashboard to enable them to be able to **monitor key company metrics**.

When you get right down to it, the cost of implementing and maintaining a dashboard may turn out to be **a cost savings** for the company. There are probably a lot of employees who are currently spending a lot of time creating and distributing reports that contain the same information that will be provided by a dashboard.

The one key benefit that is driving most companies to implement a dashboard right now is that they view it as a tool that **will allow the company to move faster**. Companies have lost what little margin for error that they used to have when it comes to responding quickly to unpleasant surprises in their markets. The hope is that a dashboard will provide them with the ability to quickly detect changes and react faster.

What's The Secret To A Successful Dashboard?

The idea behind a dashboard is simple, **present the results of data analysis**. However, exactly how to successfully implement a dashboard is not quite so straightforward.

In the past, your senior executives including the CFO may have been content to focus only on **the high-level metrics**. This could have included such items as sales revenue and profitability. However, things have changed. Now you are going to be seeing requests to provide dashboard access to operational and tactical metrics such as activities in individual accounts.

From an IT perspective, the focus is going to be on what kind of tool you'll be able to deliver. The goal is going to be to create something that will be able to take in large quantities of raw company data and then transform it into useful, actionable information **in a timeframe that meets the company's needs**.

The ultimate goal here is going to be for you to create a dashboard that is able to **combine the worlds of finance and the world of operations**. The company's needs are going to continue to evolve as your management gains experience with the dashboard. They won't truly know what they want until you present them with something that they can use and which will allow them to refine their needs and desires.

What Does All Of This Mean For You?

Every firm is in the process of trying to wade through **a flood of data**. They know that the information that they need is in there, it's just a matter of finding it that is the trick. The arrival of information dashboards may be the solution that everyone has been looking for and it may be a great opportunity to show the rest of the company the importance of information technology in solving this kind of problem.

CIOs need to work closely with their CFOs in order to determine **the company's exact needs** from its dashboard. Financial metrics are a given, but the question is what if any operational metrics are going to be needed?

In the end, the most important thing that a dashboard needs to be able to do is to allow a company to **more quickly react** to changing market conditions. A CIO who can provide his or her CFO with such a tool will be worth their weight in gold!

Chapter 5

How CIOs Can Make Social Media Work For Them, Not Against Them

Chapter 5: How CIOs Can Make Social Media Work For Them, Not Against Them

What? **Yet another social media tool has just shown up?** Between Facebook, Twitter, Tumbler, etc. is there any way that a CIO can keep on top of this fast changing area? For that matter, would it ever be possible for a CIO to find a way to harness the power of social media in order to become more productive and improve how the IT department is being managed?

Become A Channel Changer

As you may have guessed by now, the major problem with being a CIO is not that you don't have enough information, but rather that **you are deluged with too much information** in the form of emails, Instant Messages, and plain old printed memos. Unfortunately, this is so common that it's almost a part of the definition of information technology. There has to be a better way.

It turns out that the answer to this problem may come from **social media**. That online tool that has being getting so much press lately, Twitter, could be the best way for to you get the information that you need and to cut out all of the other distractions.

Here's how it would work. You'd need to set up a new Twitter account just for **your high priority communications**. Set this account to follow all of the Twitter accounts of the people who report to you. Also follow any of your key clients and your trusted colleagues from across the business.

Once you've done this, tell all of these people that the best way to get in touch with you is via sending you a Twitter direct message. You can even download the Twitter app to your smartphone and configure it so that Twitter direct messages **show up in real time**.

What you are going to find is that when the people who are trying to contact you are limited to only being able to send you 140 character messages, they are forced to **get to the point much quicker**. You'll get the information that you need, when you need it, and how you need it.

Link Up With Your CIO Friends

They say that no man is an island. It turns out that no CIO is an island either. In order to grow and improve as a CIO you are **going to need a support network** of other CIOs and peers who work in the IT sector. The question is how best to set this network up?

This means that you've got to identify 5-15 people that you want to have provide you with guidance and direction in your career. After you've identified them, **start to follow them** using the various social media tools that you have. Create Google+ circles, Facebook friends lists, and Twitter lists.

This is the group of people **whose status you will want to stay on top of**. Make sure that that you reach out to them when you encounter a tricky situation or when you are facing a specific challenge. If you know what's going on in their life, then you'll be able to determine who is available to help you out.

What All Of This Means For You

All of the new social media tools that have shown up lately are **a mixed blessing**. They are great ways communicate; however, they can contribute to the sense of being overloaded that CIOs are already feeling.

If as a CIO you can find ways to **harness the power of social media**, then you can take control of how people communicate with you. Setting up a private Twitter account is one way to provide immediate access to you to a limited set of people. Taking the time to follow a small group of your peers is a fantastic way to stay in touch with them and to make sure that they'll be there when you need their help.

Social media is something that won't be going away. CIOs need to find ways to make social media work for them, not against them so that they can show the rest of the company the importance of information technology. Use these suggestions and see if getting "plugged in" helps you to do your job better.

Chapter 6

CIOs Need To Help Workers To "Like" Their Jobs More

Chapter 6: CIOs Need To Help Workers To "Like" Their Jobs More

I've got a quick question for you: **what's the most popular site on the web?** If you said "Facebook", then I think that you'd be correct. Almost without exception, each and every person at your company may be visiting this site at least once each day to tell their friends what they've been up to. If only there was some way to capture the excitement and power of Facebook and find a way to apply it to the work that your company's employees do every day. Oh wait, there is!

What's The Big Deal About Social Networking?

Just how popular is that Facebook thing? They have as of last count **800M active users!** Clearly we humans have a need to connect and share status information that Facebook has very cleverly filled for us. It turns out that the same need exists where we work.

Pretty much since businesses were first created, the folks who run the place, including CIOs, have been looking for ways to harness the importance of information technology in order to get their employees to **share more information with each other**. The thinking goes that the more that you know about what others are doing, the better you'll be able to do your job.

Traditionally, **we've been using email to try to accomplish this**. However, as we all know that doesn't work out all that well. We get behind in our email and we can't seem to get caught up while things keep changing faster than email would ever allow us to keep up with.

It has been a part of the CIO job to be on top of this need for a number of years now. I'm not sure what the first solution was, but I'd be willing to bet that it had something to do with bulletin boards and thumbtacks. In recent years, CIOs and their IT departments have tried a number of different solutions including Wikis and blogs. **These solutions have met with mixed success** – they really require someone to be dedicated to working on them in order for them to have any real value.

Facebook has changed all of this. Now your company's workers have been taught by Facebook how to keep their status updated all the time. They know how to set up their own profile, how to form groups, and how they can "follow" other people's status updates.

Best Practices For Social Networking At Work

Why not sign everyone in the office up for Facebook and then be done with it? Well, ok, for a whole bunch of reasons including **personal privacy** and keeping control over your company's proprietary information that would not be the right thing to do.

I've got some good news for you: **there are commercial Facebook alternatives**. These include solutions from Yammer Inc., Tibco Software Inc., and Salesforce.com Inc.

As with all software tools, you can't just install the software and hope that this will solve every communication problem that your company has been having. Instead, you are going to have to give your company's employees **a bit of a nudge** in the right direction in order to make this a success.

One of **the key "lessons learned"** that is coming back from firms that have already implemented their own in-house social networking solution is to make sure to leverage the power of groups. An individual user of a social networking solution only has so much value; however, if you make that person a part of one or more groups then suddenly they become a key part of the company's success.

Groups can be automatically set up and people can be assigned by the IT department – teams, departments, branches, divisions, business units, etc. However, you are also going to want to **put the power** to both create groups and to join groups into the hands of your end users. They'll naturally form their own groups in order to tackle problems and stay on top of situations that develop.

Another key success factor has to do with who uses the company's social networking service. The answer has to include **the company's senior management**. As the workers start to become aware that the people who are running the company are both using and monitoring the new workplace social networking system, they'll get the message that this is the way that business is going to be done going forward. They'll start to use it more and that's when things will really take off!

What All Of This Means For You

In order for your company to compete in the modern global economy, you are going to need to **have every employee contributing to your success**. In order to make this happen, you'll need to find a way to allow all of your employees to communicate with each other seamlessly.

Facebook has shown CIOs the way: **it's all about social networking**. Since using Facebook at work is not an option, commercial alternatives are available. Once implemented, CIOs need to make sure that they leverage the power of groups and that they make sure that the company's senior managers use the new social networking tool.

We are just at the start of a new way to exchange information within the company. Not all of the rules are in place yet, you need to use your CIO position to be **out in front and leading the charge**. Now get out there and make sure that everyone "likes" everyone else!

Chapter 7

---

5 Secrets A CIO Needs To Know In Order To Create A Social Media Plan

Chapter 7: 5 Secrets A CIO Needs To Know In Order To Create A Social Media Plan

Darn that social media stuff! Just when you thought that the job of being a CIO **couldn't get any tougher**, along comes this whole new way for the world to communicate. The arrival of social media has just boosted the importance of information technology. What makes things even tougher is that the rest of the company is waiting for you to tell them what the rules for using social media at work is...

Let's Have A Policy Party

Hopefully by now you realize that as part of your CIO job you need to be responsible for **creating a social media policy for your company**. This policy needs to provide direction to everyone in the company to let them know what is and what is not permitted when they use social media on the job.

Just creating a policy is not enough. You are going to have to go one step further. You need to make sure that everyone **knows that the company has a policy** and just what is contained in that policy. This means that you need to get the word out and you need to collect some indication from each employee that shows that they've read the policy.

What 5 Rules Need To Be A Part Of Your Social Media Policy?

Now that you know that you need a social media policy, here comes the really big question. **What needs to go into this policy?** Depending on the industry that your company is a part of, you may already have a number of regulations about what your employees can and cannot say publically (healthcare and financial firms know all about this). However, here are 5 rules that need to be a part of every CIO's social media policy:

1. **Record Keeping:** Hopefully this is a no-brainer. Every interaction with a social media site needs to be recorded just in case there is an issue down the road.

2. **Suitability:** Your employees are going to have to be very careful when it comes to making recommendations via social media. The rules say that they can't make any recommendations via social media that they wouldn't make using the more traditional forms of communication.

3. **What Needs To Be Approved?:** The answer to this question is the key to your firm's social media participation. The right answer is that any static social media material such as profiles needs to be approved. However, the day-to-day dynamic interaction does not need to be approved.

4. **Supervision:** There always needs to be a lifeguard on duty. All of your company's social media interactions need to be supervised. The goal of this supervision should not be to crush creativity, but rather to make sure that the posters stay within the company's social media guidelines.

5. **Be Aware Of 3rd Party Posts:** It turns out that you are not responsible for any 3rd party posts that show up on your corporate sites that permit such postings. However, you do need to be aware of what is being placed there just in case you find yourself being asked how something came to be on your site.

What All Of This Means For You

The CIO position is challenging enough without having to worry about the brave new world of social media. However, social media has arrived and that means that the rest of the company needs you to step up and **tell them what the new rules are**.

The correct thing to do is to **create a company-wide policy** that will let every employee know what the rules are when it comes to interacting with the outside world via social media. This social media policy needs to include rules that describe such things as record keeping, suitability, approvals, supervision, and how you want to handle 3rd party posts.

CIOs need to understand that social media does not appear to be going away – it's here to stay. This means that **the CIO is on the front lines** of helping his or her company prepare to make the most of this new tool while preventing it from harming itself. This isn't going to be easy, but get the right social media policy in place and you'll be ahead of the curve…

Chapter 8

5 Ways That CIOs Can Do A Better Job Of Communicating In The Office

Chapter 8: 5 Ways That CIOs Can Do A Better Job Of Communicating In The Office

In the 21st Century, all business seems to be done globally. However, in order for the person with the CIO job to be effective, you are going to have to be able to communicate in the old fashion way – face to face. What this means is that you will need to **master the art of office communications** as yet another way to capture the importance of information technology. It's not impossible, but you do need to know what you are doing.

5 Tips For Communicating Well In The Office

There is no one way for you to improve your CIO communication skills in the office. Rather, what you need to do is to try out a number of different approaches and see what works best for you, your company, and your people. Here is a list of **five things** that you can do that just might help you to build some bridges between what you want people to be doing and what they actually are doing:

1. **Boost The Fun Factor:** What, you were expecting something to do with PowerPoint? Nope, it turns out that a big part of being an effective communicator in an office has to do with your ability to get everyone's attention. Finding ways to get everyone to take a break, even if it's only for 15 minutes a day or so, is a great way to get everyone to relax and to provide some face time that will allow important discussions to occur.

2. **Spend More Time Listening:** We all do a great job of looking like we are listening to what people are telling us, but are we really hearing them? In order to become an effective communicator in your office you need to be spending half of your time (or more) listening to what

people are telling you. Listening is hard work. One tip is to pretend like there will be a quiz at the end of the conversation and you need to listen well enough that you'd be able to pass the quiz.

3. **Get Rid Of The Emotions:** It's all too easy that a conversation with someone that works for you can start to turn into an attack either on you or on someone else on the team. You need to rise above this. Take the time to step back and see if you can identify where the resentment is coming from. When you are responding to the person that you're talking with, don't make it personal. Make sure that what you say as part of the conversation doesn't get taken the wrong way.

4. **Make Everyone A Business Owner:** If you want to have involved employees, then you've got to get them to feel like it's "their" company. The best way to make this happen is to create an atmosphere that lets everyone feel as though they are a business owner. There are a lot of different ways to go about doing this but being open and not keeping secrets is a good start. Allowing everyone to feel as though they have input on important decisions will go a long way in helping to boost this feeling of ownership.

5. **Trust Everyone:** This may be the hardest thing for CIOs to do. The last thing that you want to do is to be accused of micromanagement. The best way to avoid this is to start to trust the people who work for you. If you allow your people to feel that they have control over their job, then you will be allowing innovation to enter into the office. This will boost job satisfaction and will help with the overall office communication.

What All Of This Means For You

In the end, being a CIO is all about information. However, just having a piece of information will do you no good. You need to be able to communicate it to the other people who work at your company. This is going to require you to have **good office communication skills**.

How you communicate with the people who work for you will differ based on **each person's individual needs**. Some people will want to have fun in the office, some will want you to hear them. Others will be looking for you to make them feel like owners and still others will be looking for your trust. There are many different ways that you can use to reach out and connect with everyone in your IT department.

As human beings, communication is at the core of who we are. Knowing how best to communicate information to other people who work for you is a key skill for the person in the CIO position. Take the time to review this list of 5 different ways that you can **get your information across to them**. You just may find that the job of being CIO just got a lot easier!

Chapter 9

3 Tips For CIOs To Become Better Negotiators

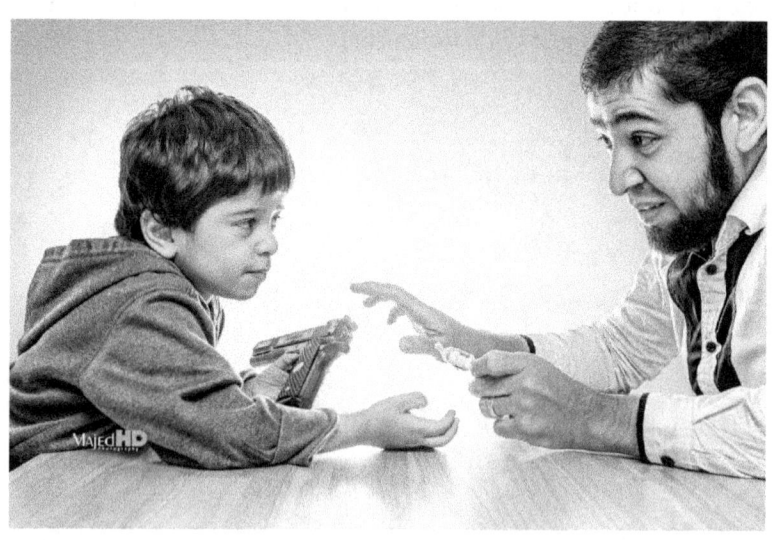

Chapter 9: 3 Tips For CIOs To Become Better Negotiators

It's interesting to realize just how important the skill of negotiating is to CIOs. Sure, we all know about the importance of information technology , but when you think about it, we spend a great deal of our time negotiating no matter if it is with vendors, other departments, or even members of our IT team. Since we do so much of this, we should always be looking **for ways to get better at it...**

3 Ways To Become A Better Negotiator

First off, when we dive into a negotiation be it with a vendor or with someone who works for our firm, all too often we just start things off with **a vague idea about what we'd like to accomplish**. We know that we need to create a deal, but we're not 100% sure what that deal is going to look like. However, we believe that we'll recognize it when we see it.

What this mean to you as the person with the CIO job is that before your next negotiation starts, **you really need to do some homework**. By taking the time to prepare for a negotiation, you'll have an advantage over the person that you'll be negotiating with. Doing your homework can be as simple as coming up with a plan for what you want to propose to the other side. When you do this, the next step is for you to highlight the key details in your plan that you want to make sure that are part of the deal that you reach.

When we are negotiating with someone, all too often it can be easy **to assume that they have more power than they really do**. They may represent a big company or a powerful internal department. We need to take a step back and realize that they are just a peer – no more, and no less. If you can see them as someone just like you, it can remove a great deal of the intimidation that they may be presenting to you and you can focus on getting what you want from them.

Finally, don't worry if **what you are asking for has never been done before**. Hey, there always has to be a first time, right? Make your case and explain to the other side how things will work. If they still seem nervous about agreeing to a deal, you can create checkpoints that will allow them to determine if the deal is being implemented in the way that they agreed to.

What All Of This Means For You

At the heart of what it means to be in the CIO position is **the ability to communicate well**. One form of communication that we all need to take the time to master is that of negotiation. Since we negotiate so often and with so many different types of people we need to get better at doing this.

There are **three ways** that we can become better negotiators. The first is to make sure that we always show up prepared to negotiate – we need to do our homework. Make sure that you see the person that you'll be negotiating with as a peer – they do not have any special powers. Finally, just because something has never been done before does not mean that it can't be done now.

As a CIO, you **never seem to have enough time to get everything done**. When you are trying to decide where to spend your time, learning to become a better negotiator is one thing that will be on your plate. Among all of the other things that you have to do, this is a good way to spend your time. Time spent becoming a better negotiator is time well invested.

Chapter 10

How Can CIOs Command The Room During A Speech?

Chapter 10: How Can CIOs Command The Room During A Speech?

One of the joys (?) of being the person with the CIO job is that **you often get asked to make speeches** where you can talk about the importance of information technology. Everyone thinks that you know what is going to happen in the future and they are hoping that if they can get you to deliver a speech, you just might let a hint of the future slip out. These are great career opportunities; however, in order to make the most of them you need to know how to command the room during your speech.

It's All About Persuasion

All too often people in the CIO position, who are technical people by their very nature, show up when it's time to give a presentation and attempt to communicate everything that they know about a topic with their audience. **Another word for this type of presentation is "dumping"**. The problem with this is that once your speech is over, nobody will be able to remember what you said.

A much better way to organize your speech is by starting out your speech by **discussing the problem that has to be solved**. No matter if you are talking about mobile products in the workplace or a new ERP solution, everything in IT is designed to solve a problem and you should start by talking about that problem.

The goal of any CIO speech should be to get your audience to either do something differently or think about something differently. You are going to want to structure your speech so that **you can persuade your audience to change**. Make sure that you deliver your information in a way that makes sense to your audience.

Does Anyone Have A Question?

As good of a speaker as you are, **there will always be questions about what you are saying** from your audience. In order to maximize the impact of your speech, you are going to want to provide your audience with an opportunity to ask you questions.

The traditional way to go about doing this is to leave time at the end of your speech to **permit your audience to ask questions**. However, it turns out that this might not be the best way to go about doing this. The reason is because studies have shown that adults have an attention span of about 20 minutes. This means that your 45-60 minute speech is going to cover at least two adult attention spans.

A much better way to deal with questions is to stop at about 20 minutes and 40 minutes into your speech and ask if there are any questions. This shakes things up, grabs people's attention, and keeps their interest. It also allows you to control how your speech ends. You don't have to take questions at the end and you can finish on a high note, not a bad or awkward question.

Beware Of The Slide Trap

I love PowerPoint, you love PowerPoint, we all love PowerPoint. All too often we are in a rush when we've been asked to give a speech and we end up throwing our slides together at the last minute. When we do this, we're often not quite sure what we are planning on saying.

When we find ourselves in this situation, we stop looking at our audience during our presentation and we start to look at the screen where our slides are being displayed. We have to do this because we're not sure what comes next. However, by doing this we lose contact with our audience.

One additional downside to looking at our slides while we talk is that our hand gestures are made towards the screen. Studies have shown that your audience will only be interested in motions made towards them. When you direct your motions towards the screen, you are giving them permission to start to ignore you.

What All Of This Means For You

One of the most important skills that a CIO must have is the ability to communicate well. This skill becomes critical when we are called upon to deliver a speech. Anyone can give a speech, only the best CIOs can command the room while they do it.

In order to command the room, first you need to make sure that you find ways to persuade your audience. Don't try to overwhelm them with too much information. Questions are always an important part of any CIO speech. Provide your audience with an opportunity to ask questions during your speech. Finally, make sure that you use PowerPoint slides effectively and don't let the slides use you.

When it comes to clearly communicating information to a group of people, giving a speech is the most effective way to accomplish this. However, as with so many things in life there is a right way and a wrong way to go about doing this. Use these suggestions to command the room the next time you are asked to give a speech.

Chapter 11

How The Orange County CTO Solved His IT Problem

Chapter 11: How The Orange County CTO Solved His IT Problem

Joel Manfredo was the CTO of Orange County, California a while ago. When he first came into office, he discovered what most CIOs discover when they start their job: **he had a lot of problems on his hands** that had nothing to do with the importance of information technology. The Orange County IT department provides IT services for over 18,000 employees who work in over 30 different government services. As Joel took over as CTO he realized that he had a bit of a mess on his hands, what was a CTO to do?

Scoping Out The Problem

When Joel Manfredo got the CIO job for Orange County the first thing that he did was to **take stock of his new responsibilities**. What he discovered was that his team was divided into two parts: full time employees and contractors. As you might imagine, within the IT department there was a great deal of conflict and they were operating inefficiently.

One of the big problems with the IT department was that **it was highly reactive**. This lead to a lot of the conflicts that it was struggling with. Joel started to fix things by bringing in a facilitator who lead meetings that were designed to show the various parts of IT how to do a better job of working with each other.

The purpose of these meetings was to **teach the IT team members accountability**. What they all need to realize was that the customer always had to come first. They had to be taught that finding ways to deliver IT services efficiently was everybody's job.

Using A Catalog To Boost Communication

Once he had the staffing situation under control, Joel moved on to looking for ways to **improve his relationship with his end users**. One of the biggest changes he implemented was to start to charge the various departments for the IT services that they were receiving. This required creating a new mind-set where users started to understand the real value of an IT service.

In order to clearly communicate the IT services that were available to the various government services, Joel had a catalog of IT services created. The purpose of creating this catalog was to provide the departments with **the ability to shop for the IT services that they needed**.

The catalog lays out each of the services that the IT department offers. Additionally, **the price of each service is detailed** as well as how the IT department charges for the service. Finally, the catalog provides tips for using each of the services that it describes.

What All Of This Means For You

Every IT department has its share of things that need to be fixed. When Joel Manfredo took over as the Orange County CTO he discovered that **he had more than his fair share of issues on his hands**.

Joel had to find a way to get his full-time employees to **work more closely with his contractors**. What he did was to create a catalog of the IT services that his department offered. This catalog was distributed to the 30 various departments that were supported by the IT department. This allowed everyone to understand what the IT department did and what new services they could request.

What Joel realized is what everyone in the CIO position needs to understand. **Clear communication is the key to running a successful IT department**. Once everyone knew what the IT department could do, they started to ask for those services and this required both sides of the IT department to start to work together much better.

Chapter 12

How CIOs Can Use Words To Boost Their Power And Credibility

Chapter 12: How CIOs Can Use Words To Boost Their Power And Credibility

As the person with the CIO job, because of the importance of information technology **your company expects a great deal from you**. However, if you have not managed to gather the power and the credibility that you are going to need in order to successfully accomplish your job, then it's going to be very hard for you to accomplish what you need to get done. What this means is that you need to discover how to boost both your power and your credibility…

Watch Your Words

There is no question that the rest of the company realizes that the CIO can play an important role in the overall success of the company. However, **it's how easy it is for the rest of the company to interact with the CIO that will go a long way in determining how much political power you are able to gather to yourself**. Do it incorrectly and all of a sudden everything that you want to accomplish will become harder to do.

The first thing that every CIO needs to realize is that the words, acronyms, and technical talk that we all use within the world of IT **needs to stay there** – in IT. Just spend a moment and think about the words that you use when you are talking with your team: servers, cloud, API, uptime, HTML, CSS, bandwidth, router, etc. Sure, we all know what these terms mean and in fact in order to do our IT job correctly we need to use them clearly and accurately to communicate what we either are working on or are going to be working on.

However, the problem arises when we go to have discussions with other parts of the company. They have no idea what any of these terms mean. What this means for us is that if we use IT terms when we are talking with non-IT employees, we'll just end up confusing them. If we are viewed as being hard to talk to, others **will simply stop talking to us**. That's why as the CIO it is your responsibility to drop all of the IT lingo that you use within the IT department when you are talking with marketing, sales, accounting, etc. Use their vocabulary which deals with things like the bottom line, business objectives, competition, etc.

It's All About Face Time

As a CIO you will not be able to accomplish what the company expects you to get done **if you can't work closely with the rest of the company**. In order to make this happen, the burden of creating relationships with the other parts of the company falls upon your shoulders. It is not their responsibility to reach out to you, rather it is your responsibility to reach out to them.

One way to develop a deeper relationship with other leaders in your company is to **take the time to go meet with them face-to-face**. All too often CIOs can find themselves hiding behind a wall of emails, texts, and perhaps even video conferences. The best (and perhaps the only) way to really connect with someone is to get out from behind your desk and go spend some quality time with them.

There are a lot of different ways to go about doing this. One of the simplest is to **offer to take other members of the company's leadership out to lunch**. If they accept your offer, then you need to make it happen. Besides eating and drinking with them, use this time to dive deeper into what their issues are. What are the challenges that their part of the company is facing right now? What kind of help do they need? If you can gather this type of information, then you'll be in a better position to have the IT department do what it is supposed to do – make the rest of the company run faster and better.

What All Of This Means For You

Knowing your technology and how to manage technical professionals are important parts of being a successful CIO. However, no CIO is an island and this means that **you need to be able to work with the rest of the company in order to accomplish all of the things that are expected of you**. What this means is that you are going to need to find ways to boost both your power and your credibility.

Since you are in the CIO position, **you are the one who is going to have to change** – the rest of the company won't change to accommodate you. The first thing that you need to realize is that your IT vocabulary is something that will hold you back. Stop using IT terms and start using the business terms that the rest of the company uses. Also take the time to meet face-to-face with other parts of the business so that they know who you are and you know how they think.

A cell phone is of no use unless it's been charged. **A CIO is of no use unless he or she has power**. Power won't be handed to you and so you'll need to take steps to get the power that you'll need. Follow these suggestions and you'll be able to accomplish all of the things that the company needs you to do.

It's from the forge of failure that the steel of success is formed.

Hard Work Does Not Guarantee Success, But Success Does Not Happen Without Hard Work.

- Dr. Jim Anderson

Create IT Departments That Are Productive And A Valuable Asset To The Rest Of The Company !

Dr. Jim Anderson is available to provide training and coaching on the topics that are the most important to people who have to manage IT departments: how can I build a productive IT department (and keep it together) while at the same time providing the rest of the company with the IT services that they need?

Dr. Anderson believes that in order to both learn and remember what he says, speakers need to laugh. Each one of his speeches is full of fun and humor so that what he says "sticks" with everyone.

Dr. Anderson's CIO SkillsTraining Includes:

4. How to identify and attract the right type of IT workers to your IT department.
5. How to build relationships with the company's senior management in order to get the support that you need?
6. How to stay on top of changing technology and security issues so that you never get surprised?

Dr. Jim Anderson works with over 100 customers per year. To invite Dr. Anderson to work with you, contact him at:

Phone: 813-418-6970 or
Email: jim@BlueElephantConsulting.com

Photo Credits:

Cover - Eirik Solheim
https://www.flickr.com/photos/eirikso/

Chapter 1: AJC1
https://www.flickr.com/photos/ajc1/

Chapter 2: Twitter
https://twitter.com/zynga

Chapter 3: Andrea Incalza
https://www.flickr.com/photos/cetaceo/

Chapter 4: Robert Couse-Baker
https://www.flickr.com/photos/29233640@N07/

Chapter 5: Jason Howie
https://www.flickr.com/photos/jasonahowie/

Chapter 6: Prachatai
https://www.flickr.com/photos/prachatai/

Chapter 7: marcmo
https://www.flickr.com/photos/marcmos/

Chapter 8: 泰德
https://www.flickr.com/photos/ted_lee/

Chapter 9: Majed Alqoyani
https://www.flickr.com/photos/majedhd/

Chapter 10: Joe Goldberg
https://www.flickr.com/photos/goldberg/

Chapter 11: Orange County Archives
https://www.flickr.com/photos/ocarchives/

Chapter 12: underclasscameraman
https://www.flickr.com/photos/underclasscameraman/

Other Books By The Author

Product Management

- How Product Managers Can Learn To Understand Their Customers: Techniques For Product Managers To Better Understand What Their Customers Really Want

- Product Management Secrets: Techniques For Product Managers To Boost Product Sales And Increase Customer Satisfaction

- Product Development Lessons For Product Managers: How Product Managers Can Create Successful Products

- Customer Lessons For Product Managers: Techniques For Product Managers To Better Understand What Their Customers Really Want

- Product Failure Lessons For Product Managers: Examples Of Products That Have Failed For Product Managers To Learn From

- Communication Skills For Product Managers: The Communication Skills That Product Managers Need

To Know How To Use In Order To Have A Successful Product

- How To Have A Successful Product Manager Career: The Things That You Need To Be Doing TODAY In Order To Have A Successful Product Manager Career

- Product Manager Product Success: How to keep your product on track and make it become a success

Public Speaking

- How To Create A Speech That Will Be Remembered

- Secrets To Organizing A Speech For Maximum Impact: How to put together a speech that will capture and hold your audience's attention

- How To Become A Better Speaker By Changing How You Speak: Change techniques that will transform a speech into a memorable event

- How To Give A Great Presentation: Presentation techniques that will transform a speech into a memorable event

- How To Rehearse In Order To Give The Perfect Speech: How to effectively rehearse your next speech to that your message be remembered forever!

- Secrets To Creating The Perfect Speech: How to create a speech that will make your message be remembered forever!

- Secrets To Organizing The Perfect Speech: How to organize the best speech of your life!

- Secrets To Planning The Perfect Speech: How to plan to give the best speech of your life

- How To Show What You Mean During A Presentation: How to use visual techniques to transform a speech into a memorable event

CIO Skills

- What CIOs Need To Know About Working With Partners: Techniques For CIOs To Use In Order To Be Able To Successfully Work With Partners

- Critical CIO Management Skills: Decision Making Skills That Every CIO Needs To Have In Order To Be Able To Make The Right Choices

- How CIOs Can Make Innovation Happen: Tips And Techniques For CIOs To Use In Order To Make Innovation Happen In Their IT Department

- CIO Communication Skills Secrets: Tips And Techniques For CIOs To Use In Order To Become Better Communicators

- Managing Your CIO Career: Steps That CIOs Have To Take In Order To Have A Long And Successful Career

- CIO Business Skills: How CIOs can work effectively with the rest of the company!

IT Manager Skills

- Growing Your CIO Career: How CIOs Can Work With The Entire Company In Order To Be Successful

- How IT Managers Can Make Innovation Happen: Tips And Techniques For IT Managers To Use In Order To Make Innovation Happen In Their Teams

- Staffing Skills IT Managers Must Have: Tips And Techniques That IT Managers Can Use In Order To Correctly Staff Their Teams

- Secrets Of Effective Leadership For IT Managers: Tips And Techniques That IT Managers Can Use In Order To Develop Leadership Skills

- IT Manager Career Secrets: Tips And Techniques That IT Managers Can Use In Order To Have A Successful Career

- IT Manager Budgeting Skills: How IT Managers Can Request, Manage, Use, And Track Their Funding

- Secrets Of Managing Budgets: What IT Managers Need To Know In Order To Understand How Their Company Uses Money

Negotiating

- Learn How To Signal In Your Next Negotiation: How To Develop The Skill Of Effective Signaling In A Negotiation In Order To Get The Best Possible Outcome

- Learn The Skill Of Exploring In A Negotiation: How To Develop The Skill Of Exploring What Is Possible In A Negotiation In Order To Reach The Best Possible Deal

- Learn How To Argue In Your Next Negotiation: How To Develop The Skill Of Effective Arguing In A Negotiation In Order To Get The Best Possible Outcome|

- How To Open Your Next Negotiation: How To Start A Negotiation In Order To Get The Best Possible Outcome

- Preparing For Your Next Negotiation: What You Need To Do BEFORE A Negotiation Starts In Order To Get The Best Possible Deal

- Learn How To Package Trades In Your Next Negotiation

- All Good Things Come To An End: How To Close A Negotiation - How To Develop The Skill Of Closing In Order To Get The Best Possible Outcome From A Negotiation

Miscellaneous

- The Internet-Enabled Successful School District Superintendent: How To Use The Internet To Boost Parental Involvement In Your Schools

- Power Distribution Unit (PDU) Secrets: What Everyone Who Works In A Data Center Needs To Know!

- Making The Jump: How To Land Your Dream Job When You Get Out Of College!

- How To Use The Internet To Create Successful Students And Involved Parents

Your Success As A CIO Depends On How Well You Communicate

This book has been written with one goal in mind – to show you how you can become a CIO who communicates clearly. It's not easy being a CIO so we're going to show you what you need to be doing in order to sure that everyone understands what needs to be done!

Let's Make Your CIO Career A Success!

What You'll Find Inside:

- **CIOS SHOULD STOP SENDING EMAILS – NOW!**

- **CIO LESSONS FROM ZYNGA: DON'T MANAGE LIKE THEY DO!**

- **WHAT A CIO NEEDS TO KNOW ABOUT CREATING A TWITTER STRATEGY**

- **HOW CIOS CAN MAKE SOCIAL MEDIA WORK FOR THEM, NOT AGAINST THEM**

Dr. Jim Anderson brings his 25 years of real-world experience to this book. He's been a senior IT executive at some of the world's largest firms. He's going to show you what you need to do (and not do!) in order to make your CIO career a success!

www.ingramcontent.com/pod-product-compliance
Lightning Source LLC
Chambersburg PA
CBHW060416190526
45169CB00002B/918